THIS WEIGHT OF LIGHT

Also by Chris Powici

Somehow This Earth
(Diehard Poetry, 2009)

THIS WEIGHT OF LIGHT

Poems

Chris Powici

RED SQUIRREL PRESS

First published in the United Kingdom in 2015
by Red Squirrel Press
www.redsquirrelpress.com

Red Squirrel Press is distributed by Central Books Ltd.
and represented by Inpress Ltd.
www.inpressbooks.co.uk

Designed and typeset by Gerry Cambridge
www.gerrycambridge.com

A CIP catalogue record is available from the British Library.

ISBN: 978 1 910437 10 0

Printed in the UK by Martins the Printers Ltd. on acid-free paper
sourced from mills with FSC chain of custody
certification. www.martinstheprinters.com

CONTENTS

For Helen Lamb and Angus Dunn
these northern words.

THE OTTER GODDESS

The otter goddess won't hear our prayers,
cares more about the sway and feel
of kelp against her belly
than whether we believe in her or not.

She'd sooner eat gull than have anything to do
with love or forgiveness;
she can't even tell herself apart
from the sinewy crab huntress
her presence inhabits.

All she knows is grace –
cool thrill of tail-flick and fur-glitter
as she surges up the green depths
to sashay on the swell.

And guillemots dive about her.
And death is another time.

FLIGHTS

one heron is a slow thrown spear

siskin are god-motes
twisting in a yellow wind

peewits are Stukas in love

skein-shapes of the pinkfoot
are longbows drawn
and longbows shot and trembling
harps, rivers, the knot in your heart unravelled
your heart's blood streaming

and billowing in the tractor's wake
gulls are spindrift
gulls are snow

THE TOWN

I sit at my window and there are wolves
coming down the street, wolves sidling past
bus shelters and news-stands,
rubbing their backs against pub walls
and parked cars, sniffing the rainy air
and leaving their piss steaming in pools
outside laundrettes and takeaways.

And there are people
coming from shoe shops and cafés
department stores and banks,
passing between the wolves
and hurrying through the rain
down other streets,
streets of lamplight and leaf fall,
to paths of stone and doors of wood.

GLEN EINICH

Like bone singing, Am Beanaidh breaks from its loch
in flashes and splinters, quickens to a bright yell
in the dry September heather.

Dippers flit between loud stones
and the gamekeeper's pointers wander the river's
flickering edge, breathing hotly, dripping light.

Meanwhile the pines, those gaunt brethren,
keep their thrawn, dark-rooted peace
go on drinking.

THE HARE

leaps out of the yellowing
may gorse

lollops down tractor ruts
almost to the gate

and just sits there
all bristle and haunch

king of the grass
and all this gorse-bright earth

giving me its dark
god-eyed stare

COWS AT NIGHT

hooves splosh the mud by the gate
up from the gut's well
serene heavy rumbles of cuddy air
ripple and echo
like small grass-scented thunderstorms
and loose mists of breath rise
halfway the height
of the whitethorn hedge
then hang   drift
making and unmaking the world

DEER

in the dawn light
on the cold hill
the deer are running

the thud of their hooves
on the bed of the stream
is the drum that rocks
the roots of the birch
and the wind that shakes
the birch tree's leaves

rain is their tribe song
rain is their robe

snow is the dust
of the bones of deer
falling to earth

and earth is the dark
deep silence of things
where you dream yourself
human, alive
watching the red deer running
on the wall of a cave

BULLOCK

A thing of bone and rain and skin
the colour of birdshit and dead heather
the Braes of Doune bullock's sunk
to its shins in grass and mud –
its only business in these high, cold hills
to stare at you, and stare at you
and stand its ground forever.

MAY BIKE RIDE

All day long a raw eyeball-freezing wind
screaming down the coast
too brute cold to stand more than twenty minutes
at the Rhue lighthouse watching the gannets wheel and dive
before you're pedalling back up the hill, heavy and hunched
into mean blasts of sleety rain
when a weasel pokes its pointy fierce head
through the bars of a cattle grid
wild and ridiculous as a prize-winning slimmer escaping Alcatraz
so you brake, twist round in the saddle
catch a blear of arse and tail hurtling into the gorse
and on the other side of Loch Broom
the sheer heathery mass of Bheinn Ghoblach
rising through wind-torn cloud into utter light
so real, so high, so like the only mountain there has ever been
suddenly you want this shitty bastard no-spring-at-all
to stay and stay and stay.

AUGUST

My father is kneeling in a scatter of carrot and potato leaves
in the vegetable patch at the back of the garden.
He has just flipped the stub of his Kensitas onto the compost heap
and his trowel lies beside him on the dry earth.
Soon he will come indoors to drink tea and read *The People*.
But for now he is still, watching the evening's first pipistrelles
work the lush, familiar air.
So I imagine.

TREESTRUCK

If not last week's blazing autumn maple
half a mile beyond the Dalbrack cattle grid
so crammed with pipits
there seemed more birds than leaves
the great shivering swell of it
more song than tree,
I'll go back forty years and more
to that fat pagan oak
across the field from the Moggy Pond
all galls and holes, anyone could slip
a black-plimsolled foot into the wounded bark
shimmy up the trunk
and stand slap-bang in the middle
of the belly of the witch
knee-grazed and grinning
under the flood of sky.

WILLOW

24th January, 5am, faint shine of streetlight and frost
glazing the black bark and half the eastern sky cradled
in its thin branches, my neighbour's bare wee tree's
become a star-cracked vase brimming with night
and god knows what nebulae and rush
of strange dark matter trembling on the lip

OAK

these hundred thousand sun-hammered leaves
this weight of light

SHERIFFMUIR

Bracken Dying

Bracken, dying, turns
the colour of cattle-trough water
a cow's eye
the almost darkness
of a Blackford field
in the late October dusk
before the rain has cleared
before the stars.

Ewe Skull

Between the curlew's nest
and moor stream's stony rush
this small white death;

faded radiance of fox-licked bone
sunk in ling and flecked by spits of rain
drifting inland on a faint sea-wind.

Little Corum

sheer january rain

the moor grass leans toward you
in low, stiff waves

between clouds
hills come and go
like whales

Ochil Blizzard

Nothing is happening except snow
settling on the scrawny mesh
of deer-fence wire and sitka branches.

Snowed-under 4x4 tracks fade
into the lush blur of the wood.

The sky is nowhere.
All distances are ghosts.

Greenloaning

The Ochils, midsummer, and no telling
the raincloud from the rain;

dark plantation spruce loom
through the smirr

blackface sheep plunge wearily
into the high bracken

and soft moon-coloured cattle
stand drenched and silent
half in grass, half in sky.

Harperstone

Crap-stained, straggly as drunks,
bleating, panicked sheep
pour into ditches
slam against fences
swirl round on themselves
heads and hooves flooding
the black tarmac
the sunlit grass.

Lapwings at Sheriffmuir

impossible
that the sheer split
second grace of their love-
dives could end
in anything
but blood
feather bone
speckling
the wet grass
of the killing
ground

that they could aim
themselves at death
headlong
wings bent
intent as suicides
and at the last

moment
rise

through
thin rain
to the low moor
sky crying
their lives
like nothing
on this grave
earth

Bracken Rising

peewits tumble and flounce
over the dark ploughed earth

curlew, somewhere,
are flinging cry after cry
into the blue day

and in a ditch by Drumcairn
out of the tangled dead
winter stalks
tiny, unstoppable
this green push

MILES

Nineteen years after the death of my father I'm cycling
through a crowd of twisted scots pines on the Sheriffmuir
Road thinking about the family trip to Romania in 1970
and dad standing in a Timisoara back yard – aunts, cousins,
uncles, in-laws, fluttering madly about a rough trestle table
laden with ham, bread and homemade lemonade, thirty
years of war and exile falling away like the petals from the
cherry tree, and dad as deeply calm and happy as I've ever
seen him, as if all this din of love were the breeze from
the river or the swell of birdsong and the thought happens
that if I could look at myself right now I'd see a fifty one
year old man criss-crossed by pine shadows crammed full
of things to say and sing and speechless.

TRACKS

Victoria

headlights flowing through long London dusks
embankment trees
the quietness of rain

Richmond Park

deer look out
from the high summer grass
as if from another world

Allan Water

the hind's tracks disappear
among stones and reeds
only the river moves

Kilmory

a ledge of lichened rock
the bright cold sea
thrift, a gull feather, wind

Lamlash

the wind made flesh
in the swerve of a gull
the plainsong of tides

Dochart

in a dipper's eye
the cold ten thousand year shine
of falling water

Glen Artney

up to her neck in deer grass and thistles
the curlew's cool, long cry
trembles like a stream beginning

Arbroath

gulls on the harbour wall
streetlamps coming on
the sea unfolding like a petal

ROOKS

Four days after the funeral of my mother
I am walking up Kippendavie Road
and the June evening sky's filled
with the slow, wild cries of rooks
gliding in from the sheep fields
to the sprawl of oaks halfway up the hill.

My mother had her service all planned out
would have imagined her sons and daughters
grandchildren, neighbours
gathered on the narrow, familiar pews
as sunlight flowed through the tall windows
onto the bright cross and cut flowers –
imagined our voices joined in psalm
I will lift up mine eyes unto the hills, from whence cometh my help

but these rough midsummer hymns?
these dark stone-throated birds
vanishing into the leaves
as the earth calls them – us – all of us – home?

GEOFF

A shy man, fortyish, with thick black hair
likes a bet and works on the railways
checking tickets between Ayr and Glasgow;
has an ex-wife and daughter living in Dundee
and girlfriend, Jan, who works at the bookies
wears cut-off jeans and has a way of saying *Geoff*
that makes his name seem like a breath of summer wind
and who stays with him most weekends
at his council maisonette near the retail park
where there are thirty-seven Duke Ellington CDs
stacked beside the stereo and a photograph
of Kim, his daughter, hanging next
to a watercolour print of Shergar
on the lounge wall

and where it's a cold January morning
and he's standing at the kitchen door
shaking the breadboard free of crumbs
for the blue tits in his frozen garden
when one of them flutters to the shed roof
and beats the snowflakes from its wings
until it's more blizzard than bird
a blur of white in the dead grey air
while Geoff just stands there
spilling crumbs from the breadboard
shivering and struck
by the suddenness of love
for different bodies
different things.

SNOWS

Big late January snowflakes
settle and melt on the bare branches
of the cherry tree across the lane
while I listen to a professor on the radio
describe how the universe fizzes
with particles so magnificently strange
anything we might call *miracle* or *holy*
can't hold a candle to the extravagant reality
of muons and neutrinos shimmying on the infinite
edge of space and time.

Meanwhile it snows.
The postman arrives, treading slush
and chaffinches wander in and out
of soft explosions of sky.

IN OCTOBER, IN MONTROSE

A narrow leaf-stained street. A woman in a blue coat
stands beside a garden wall listening
to the raw salt-throated cries of 40,000 pink footed geese
surge across the mud flats into every lane and vennel
of the darkening town; a vast estuarine chorus
yelling its brute *hallelujah* to the trees and houses
shaking the very air, and then the woman
lights a cigarette and walks calmly on –
as if the holy hollering of geese is just a noise
the universe happens to make in October, in Montrose.
As if she has a million gods to choose from.

MONTROSE BASIN SEA EAGLE

Probably nothing more than a buzzard
talked-up by a tourist for the local paper
but just the thought of those vast wings
circling this borderland of mud, marsh and tide
makes you lean close to the window
of the Glasgow train, aching for a glimpse.
But the Montrose skies show no eagle
so the eye makes do with a cormorant
swooping south across the lagoon –
if the raw beautiful shock of seeing
something so finely black and quick as a cormorant
glide through the waning coastal light
can be described as *making do*.

LUNAN BAY

You knelt at the tide-edge
and built frail cairns of whelk and mussel shells.
Above the waves a wave of gulls
hung in a blue shock of September sky.
A boy roared an ancient Honda 125
between the river and the dunes.
Sand flared from the wheels, the gulls screamed

and still you probed and nudged and tweaked
as if you'd waited all your life to feel
each grit-clogged smithereen
each dirty glittering scrap
pass through your hands and become
something known, something seen.

SLIOCH

Summer three years ago I had an idea
to climb Slioch in Wester Ross
so I took a train, and another train
to Achnasheen and then the postbus
down to Kinlochewe where the path begins
among the birch and bracken beneath Beinn a' Mhuinidh
but it turned out the hottest day in years
and I gave up halfway, just as the path steepens
into Coire an Tuill Bhàin.

I lay down in the coarse grass by a slab of gneiss.
My shirt clung to my back, the air was thick with flies
but looking across Loch Maree
to the sun-broken clouds drifting south
over the high grey mass of Beinn Eighe
all I could think was:

somehow this earth
somehow this sky

RHUE

Kodie and *Angie*
cut deep into the thick white paint
of the lighthouse door.
Such fierce knife-written love – hard not to imagine
some improbably rainless Saturday night
miles from teachers and fathers
even the gulls fallen to quietness
as they scramble down the path from the car park
rip loose the padlock and chain
and in good, good time
lie still and naked under the big lamp
listening to the beat of the waves
the soft chug of a prawn boat
coming home from the Minch
and their names, barely more than breaths now,
drifting all the way to Canada
on the thousand voices of the wind.

THE HARBOUR SEAL

A seal breaks the low swell
between marker buoys, close to the pier,
breathes slow, dribbly breaths.
Its skin's a mottled oily grey
like the winter sky or mildewed glass
and though it's hard to say
if the seal's looking up at you
or the crowd of prawn boat masts hugging the dock
the small, black eyes make you think of rain
and how the earth gives itself to rain
and darkness and tides and when the seal dives
the quiet creel-heaped pier feels suddenly cold
and in the past.

FLANDERS MOSS

flat land   deep land

nothing higher than scrub birch
between you and those miles-away mountains
heat-hazed and blue in the distance

even the air feels empty, cleansed

so you look down
down through the wind-shivered seedheads
of hare's-tail bog cotton
to shallow beetle-furrowed pools
fringed by quaggy almost-islands
of deer grass and heather still to bloom

and the sheer living green of the moss itself

papillosum
magellanicum
imbricatum

infinite low-rise of sphagnum
moth-ground and adder-cradle
intricate and crowded as a city
and all of it floating
on seven thousand years of peat
the cool rich stuff of death
oozing its thick, milky mud
just a step, just a thought away

soft land   dark land

earth on the verge of becoming water
earth you could drown in

ALL THE TIME BILLIONS

all the time billions of almost nothings passing right
through us it would take four light years travelling
through solid lead for a neutrino to notice anything else
in the universe actually existed so this holy palaver of skin
bone hair etc is less than mist and the migrations of geese
plato's head bach fugues aspirin the difference engine
rainforests and the paris metro barely more than the sheen
of dust on a bat's wing who knows maybe even you yes *you*
with your blue northern eyes and memories of the sea are
flowing through this poem rapt and quantumly beyond its
trembling nest of sounds and are wrought of the very stuff
of light improbable and utter

A MOMENT OF HEAT
—for Viv

When the universe began
it was small, dark and pretty
wore its hair up
and flashed a winning smile
that lasted for all of one thousand-
millionth of a second
whereupon it splintered
like glass on fire
flew outward and cooled.

There are bits of a grin everywhere.
So they say.

Yet from this event came matter
and from that first hydrogenous matter
all other things

even the sudden involuntary image
of my father sitting where I sit now,
elbows resting on a restaurant table,
watching the evening ferry pull out
of the harbour towards the mainland lights;

even the scratched wood surface
of the table itself.

NIGHT FISHING

i.m. Les Powici

Britten's Pond, a July dusk
mayflies hazing the flat, brown water
as the day's last rooks flowed into the trees
and you threw crusts of Mother's Pride
out among the reeds where, you reckoned,
the big carp swam like slow, fat kings.

A moth-rich summer darkness came –
some mist, grass and bracken scents,
train echoes from the bridge across Salt Box Road
but all that cool, unlucky night
our hooks hung weightless, free.

I can't remember if we blamed the weather or the bait
or if we said much at all
but I can see you, Les, settled into the shadow
of that ridiculously big angler's umbrella
a mug of thermos tea cradled on your lap
while you drew calmly on a Players Number 6
as if you'd always known
it wasn't about the strike, the catch

and isn't now
talking about you, in your garden
in the April sunlight
these forty slow years later.
These other worlds.

EBB TIDE

Dunlin skitter and dab.
A tidepool puckers in a pinch of wind.
Across the strand Oronsay rises greenly
into a wet, gull-streaked sky
and for a second you half-believe
that everything that has ever lived
is living still, a cool salt mile
beyond the end of the Scalasaig road
at the rainy, late September
beginning of the world.

STONES

A week since the thaw and Feddal Pond's
still sheened in pale, dove-grey ice
that twangs and thrums with every stone
I slide across the shallows
until they form a paltry *Callanish* of muddy rock
too roughly laid to track the moon and sun
but for a few cold hours, days perhaps,
speckling this frail ground
like a fall of seed
or the stilled shadows of birds.

MERKADALE CEMETERY

Between the graves and the loch
a few cows drifting
through the high, wet grass
like a heavy breeze;
on the beach, three boats –
rudderless, keel planks cracked or missing,
what's left of their hulls
scoured grey by wind and sand
but holding to the shore
as if waiting through their own long deaths
for the dead of Skye to rise
walk a hundred yards of cattle-trodden earth
and, in their own good time, sail quietly away.

ROE

even now the sunlight
lying thickly on her back
and on the beech
and rhododendron leaves

even now the close trees
the deep air
the twitch of her hoof
on the dry earth

SHILLINGHILL

grass, flies, sun
an abandoned Bedford van
drowning in bracken

even the bracken is drowning in bracken

pipits fly up from quad tracks
make the most of a thin wind

a ram stares
through the bars of a cattle feeder
as if, suddenly, it believes
in the things of the world

as if there's no end
to the flies and the grass
no end to the sun

WESTER GLEN ALMOND

the high, hurt cry of a buzzard
a meadow pipit tweeting madly from the bracken

and the new risen Almond rolling its cold weight
by heaps of sheep-rubbed stones
leaking rain and memory

nothing lasts
everything belongs

EAST COAST STATION

It is raining and the Aberdeen train flows
over the South Esk viaduct like a long blue ghost.
Geese rise from the lagoon in their ragged thousands.

The woman standing next to me on platform 2
is wiping her glasses on a scrap of Kleenex
and shuffling from foot to foot
as if she can't decide whether to look at the radiant windows
     of the Scotrail Express
or the frantic, wing-darkened sky.

Then a fierce chorale of train brakes, goose cries, rain
and a voice on the tannoy
speaking the names of the good, wet Earth:
Montrose Stonehaven Aberdeen

IDAHO

Almost forty years after his death from cancer of the tongue
at the Calvary Hospice in New York
James Wright is telling me about a voice on the radio
mourning the endless winter daybreak of America
and I imagine miles of fencewire and snow, mountains dark with
    pines
not even a crow breaking the hard December silence
but when I put the book down and look at James' neatly bearded face
looking at me from the back cover
I think about this morning's April sunlight flooding the hills
    of Sheriffmuir
as if it had come bubbling up from the roots of the heather and grass
and I remember another of his poems, the one where a shy indian
    pony
nuzzling her head against his left hand
makes him feel he could step out of his body and 'break into blossom'
and I want to draw his ghost through whatever frontiers
of time and weather lie between us
and breathe into its ear
you said it James, you said it

OTTER

Until that rain-cool morning
cycling the sea road south from Lochranza –
and then only for a second as she surfaced, glitteringly,
through the small green waves – I'd never dreamed
an otter and the sun are the same thing
anymore than I'd dreamed the difference in time
between a bike ride and the rest of a life
isn't a question of minutes and years
but the heave of tides, animal glimpses
shifting intensities of bodies and light.

Since then the world has fallen slowly back
into place; names make sense, words seem
to know what they're talking about –
but this afternoon I stood at the kitchen window
and could feel the tongue longing to rebel:
call tree-shadows – *a dark choir shining*, crows – *blood angels*
the flow of cloud through a blue March sky –
everything there is.

JONI

I'm cycling down the Glen Road into a 9am October sun
when a wood pigeon clatters from the trees above Kiltane
and I think of the bare ruined choirs of sonnet 73
except the voice I imagine I'm hearing isn't mine
or Shakespeare's but Joni Mitchell's rising from the dark
unleafing branches like the last sweet bird on earth –
in me thou seest the twilight of such day
and even the silences between the words are so steeped
in fear and hurt that when I swerve onto the Wharry Bridge
and Joni tells me *to love that well which thou must leave ere long*
I realise it's my own death she's singing, as real as rain or air
and here, now, even as I surge through deep fallen leaves
and I'm splattered in mud and sun.

ON KERRERA

On Kerrera, at Shell Bay,
among seaweeds and stones
I'm looking across the Firth of Lorn
to Lismore and the Morven hills
and thinking about a poem I've been trying to write
describing some graves on Skye
when a cormorant breaks
black and gleaming
through the low waves
and for a cold and beautiful second
I can't remember a thing.

READING KAPLINSKI

I'm halfway through *The Wandering Border*
when I come to an image of the night sky
reflected in a bucket of well water.
The poem continues for another four lines
but already I have stopped reading;
all I can see is a rough-planked bucket
swinging on its wet chain
a big autumn moon and stars like windblown leaves
trembling in a few inches of water
everything so clear, so close
I feel as if I could dip my hands
into the shining depths of space
even when I go back to the book
and realise there's no moon, no stars
just this 'cold, colourless' liquid
and Jaan Kaplinski's face, mirrored on the surface,
waiting to drink.

OCTOBER GEESE

the autumn sun hanging
from the branches of an Ochil pine

across the road, five or six hundred greylag geese
pecking the furrowed earth
for flecks of stubble

just days ago, the greylag huddled in an Iceland marsh
sunlight breaking on peat-dark pools
snow on the hills

now the same sun burning in the trees
blue autumn sky, cool wind

the murmur of geese in a ploughed field
like prayers heard in a dream

somebody telling you this
you listening

FIRES

everything flowing, and flown:

that phone call from Les, his voice
low, creaking with cancer and love
when we talked of fishing, haplessly, for carp
some long gone July dusk

snow on a car windscreen
a blur of fields and trees
streetlamps like small fires burning

the little harbour at Drinishader
Atlantic night, rain
a lobster boat lolling on its rope
and the tide high and echoey in the bay
like a sung darkness

NOTES

Sheriffmuir

Sheriffmuir is an area of moorland in the Ochil Hills above Dunblane in Perthshire. In 1715 Jacobite and Government forces fought the Battle of Sheriffmuir. Neither side could claim outright victory; hundreds of men died. Probably lapwings lived in Sheriffmuir then as well, although there were not so many sheep.

Rooks

The quotation in italics is from Psalm 121 (the King James Version).

Flanders Moss

Flanders Moss lies at the western edge of the carse of Stirling and is one of the largest areas of lowland bog in Britain. Much of the moss is now managed as a National Nature Reserve.

Idaho

This poem contains, in adapted form, quotations from James Wright's poems 'The Frontier' and 'A Blessing'.

Fires

The phrase 'everything flowing, and flown' is adapted from a line in Elizabeth Bishop's poem 'At The Fishhouses'.

ACKNOWLEDGEMENTS

Thanks are due to the editors of the following
publications in which these poems first appeared:
*Albatross, Causeway, Into the Forest: An Anthology of Tree Poems,
Transnational Literature, New Writing Scotland, Poetry
Scotland, Poetry Map of Scotland, Smiths Knoll, Southlight, The
Dark Horse, Gutter, The Thing That Mattered Most: Scottish Poems
for Children, Scottish Poetry Library Best Scottish Poems* online.

'Flanders Moss' was written for the project *People, Peat
and Poetry* organised by Scottish Natural Heritage;
'Joni' originally appeared on the website of
Stirling Council as poem of the month, May 2014.
Versions of some of the poems were published in the
chapbook *Somehow this Earth* from Diehard Poetry.

Thanks to Helen Lamb, Richie McCaffery
and Kathleen Jamie for their wise words.